LET'S EXPLORE THE DEEP BLUE SEA

Deep sea creatures must
survive in extremely
harsh conditions, such
as hundreds of bars of
pressure, small amounts of
oxygen, very little food,
and constant extreme cold.

The Japanese
spider crab has
the greatest
leg span of
any arthropod,
reaching 12 feet
from claw to claw.
Adult Japanese
spider crab can be
found at depths
between 90 and
6,000 meters.

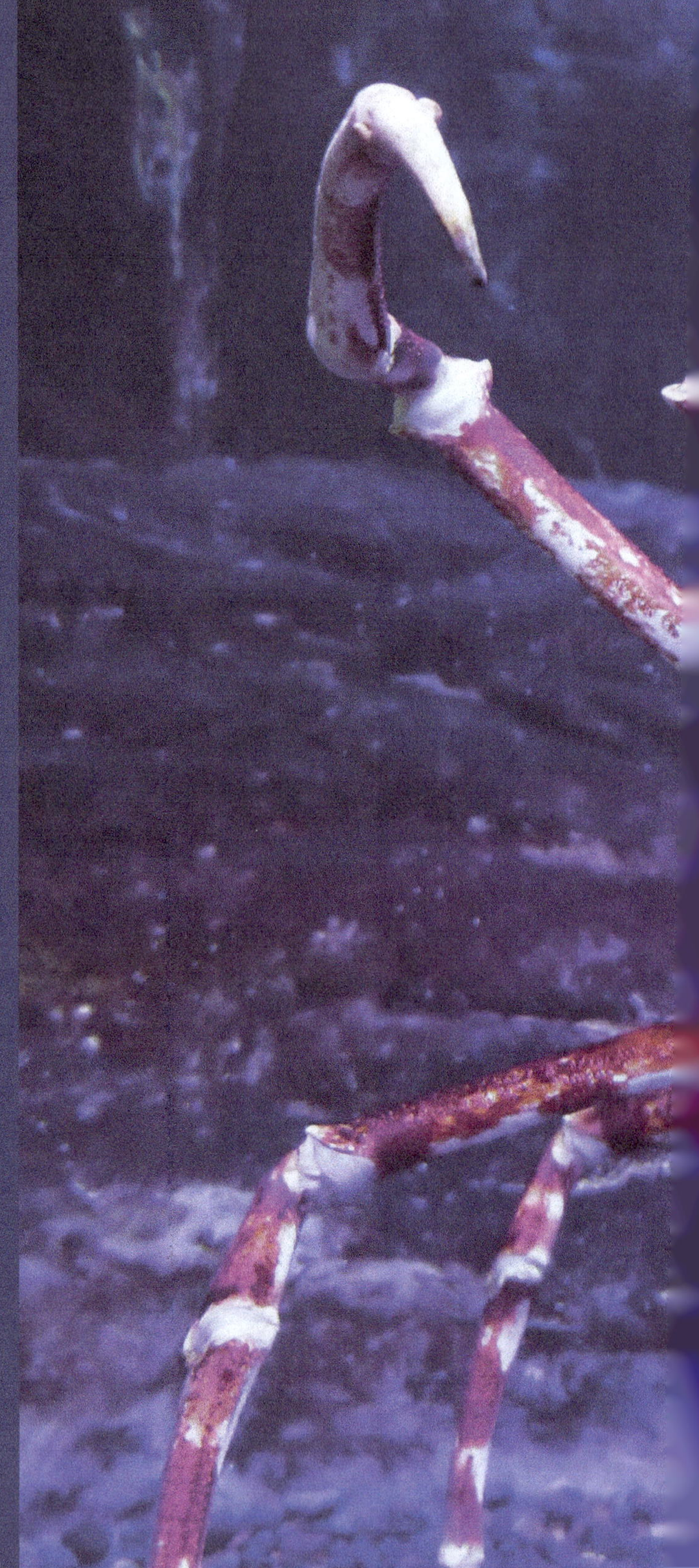

The ocean sunfish is the heaviest known bony fish in the world, with large specimens weighing nearly 5,000 pounds. Sunfish are swim at depths up to 600 meters.

A nudibranch have a shell in their larval stage, but it disappears in the adult form. Nudibranchs live at virtually all depths of salt water, from the seashore to depths of well over 700 meters.

The nautilus can reach 8 to 10 inches in diameter. Nautilus feeds on crabs and other animals, which it catches with its long, slender tentacles that encircle the mouth. The greatest depth at which a nautilus has been sighted is 703 meters.

The sperm whale is the world's largest toothed predators. Mature males average at 16 metres in length but some may reach 20.5 metres. This mammals have been recorded plunging to 2,250 metres for prey.

Moray eel have
a poor vision and
they mostly rely
on their keen
sense of smell.
Moray eel live at
depths to several
hundred metres,
where they spend
most of their time
concealed inside
crevices and
alcoves.

Jellyfish are composed of more than 90%. water. A group of jellyfish is sometimes called a bloom or a swarm. Jellyfish are found in every ocean, from the surface to the deep sea.

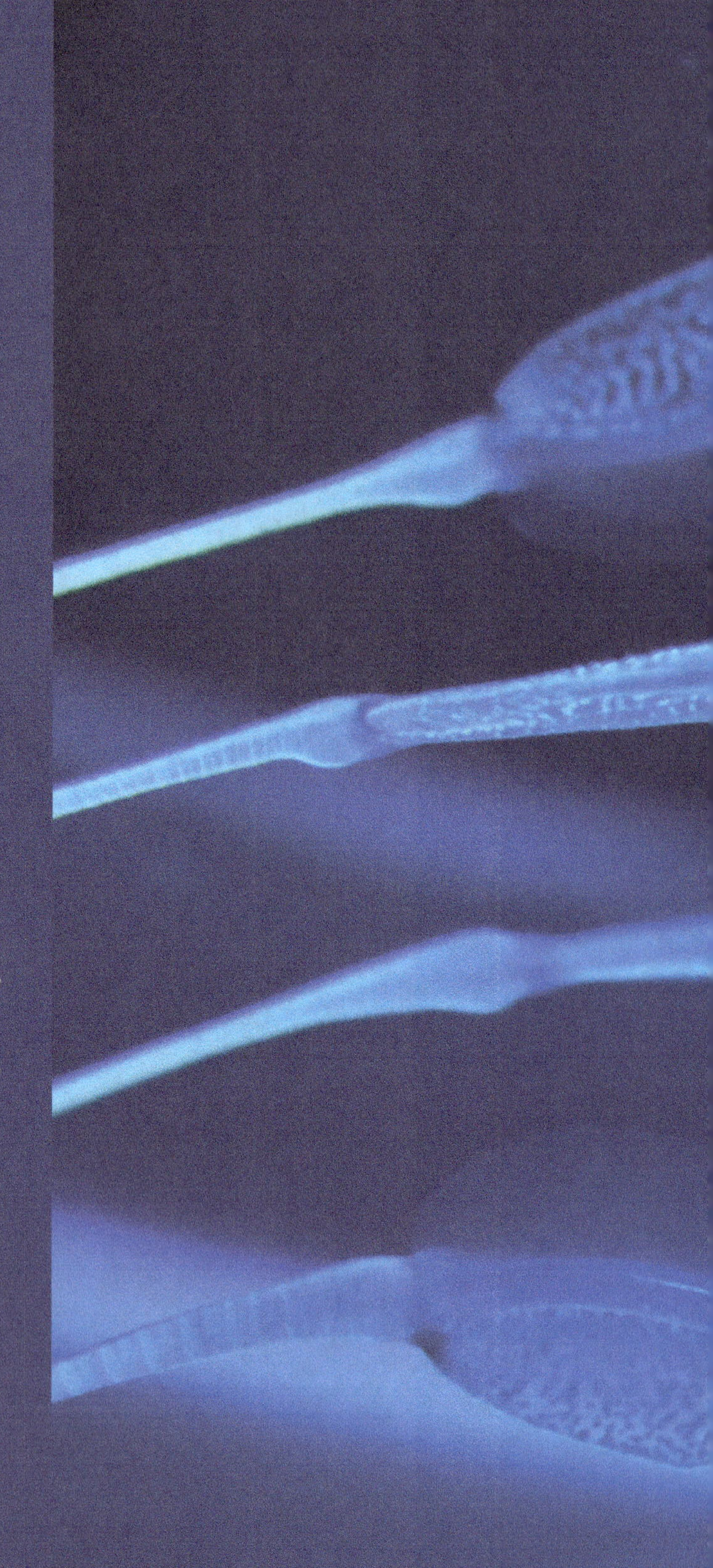

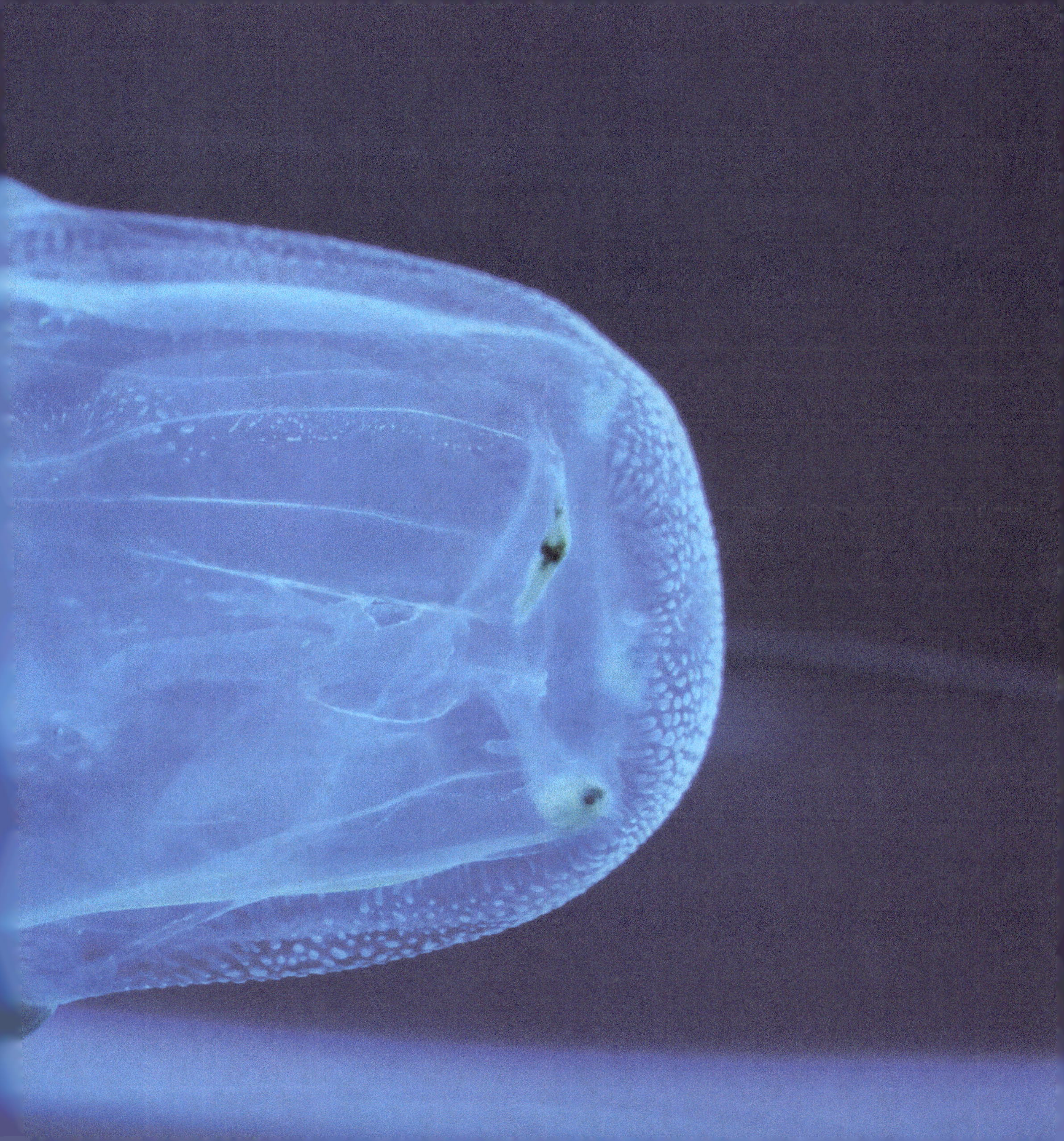

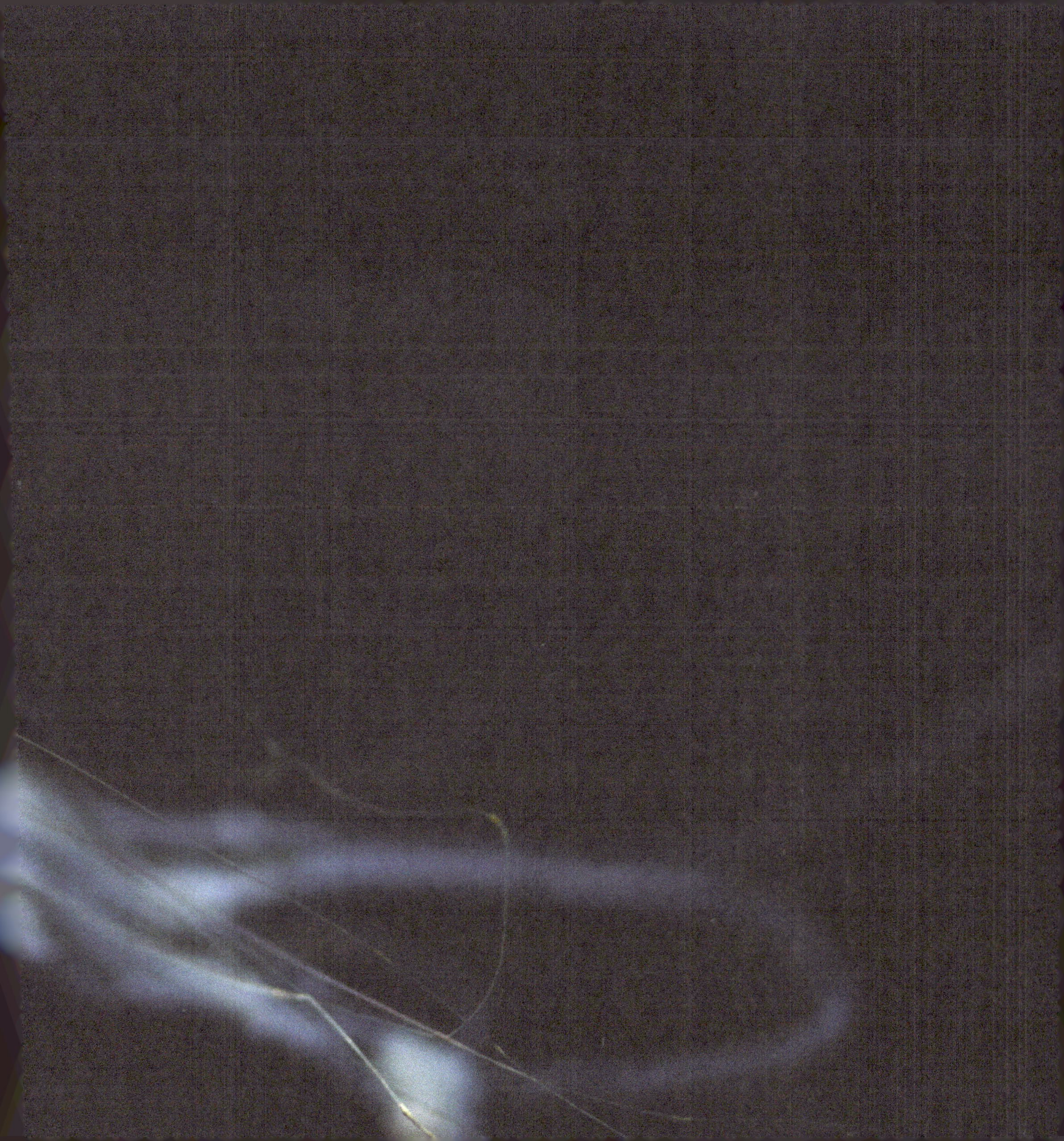

The stargazers
have the mouth,
nostrils, and eyes
set high in the
head. Stargazers
lie buried in the
sand or mud,
waiting for their
prey of small
crustaceans.